Learning English
Ausgabe A
Teil 2

Grammatisches Beiheft

Ernst Klett Verlag Stuttgart

Inhalt nach Lektionen

		Seite	§§
L 1	Kurzfragen	7	1
	Kurzfrage beim Imperativ	7	2
	so – nor – neither	7	3
L 2	Das Pronomen mit *-self*	8	4–5
	Englische Verben ohne Reflexivpronomen	8	6
	Pronomen der Gegenseitigkeit	9	7
L 3	Der Plural zusammengesetzter Substantive	9	8
	Substantive, die nur im Plural stehen	10	9
	Substantive, die nur im Singular stehen	10	10
	Verschiedene Bedeutung im Singular und Plural	10	11
	Das Geschlecht der Substantive	11	12
	Singular und Plural bei Zahlenangaben	12	13
	Possessiver Plural	12	14
L 4	Das Passiv: einfache Form und Verlaufsform	12	15
	Der Passivsatz bei Verben mit einem Objekt	13	16
	Der Passivsatz bei Verben mit zwei Objekten	13	17
	Der Infinitiv im Passiv	14	18
L 5	Die unvollständigen Hilfsverben und ihre Ersatzverben	14	19
	Der Infinitiv ohne *to*	16	20
	Der Infinitiv mit *to*	16	21
L 6	Das Adjektiv als Substantiv	16	22
	Das Adjektiv mit Stützwort	17	23
	Zahlwörter (Wiederholungszahlen; Zahlen der Reihenfolge; Zeitangaben: Gemeine Brüche; Dezimalbrüche)	17	24
	Grund- und Ordnungszahlen	18	25
	Maße und Gewichte	19	26
L 7	Notwendige und ausmalende Relativsätze	19	27
	that als Relativpronomen	19	28
	Der notwendige Relativsatz ohne Relativpronomen	20	29
	Die Nachstellung der Präposition	20	30
	Das Komma	21	31
L 8	*all*	21	32
	much, many, a lot of	21	33
	little, a little – few, a few	22	34
	no und seine Zusammensetzungen	22	35
	some und *any* und ihre Zusammensetzungen	23	36
	every – each	23	37
	Unbestimmte Pronomen (Zusammenfassung)	24	38
	what – which	24	39
L 9	Das Gerundium	25	40
	Das Gerundium im Satzzusammenhang	25	41
	Das Gerundium nach Präpositionen	26	42
	Präposition + Gerundium in der Bedeutung eines Nebensatzes	26	43

		Seite	§§

L 10	Das Partizip Präsens	27	44
	Das Partizip Perfekt mit passivem Sinn	27	45
	Das Partizip in der Bedeutung eines Nebensatzes	28	46
	Die *ing*-Form im Englischen (Überblick)	28	47
L 11	Eigennamen und Zeitbezeichnungen mit und ohne bestimmten Artikel	29	48
	Allgemeinbegriffe mit und ohne bestimmten Artikel	29	49
	Bestimmter Artikel bei näherer Bestimmung	30	50
	Redewendungen mit und ohne bestimmten Artikel	30	51
L 12	Der unbestimmte Artikel	31	52
	Nachstellung des unbestimmten Artikels	31	53
L 13	Die einfache Form und die Verlaufsform des Perfekts	32	54
	Das deutsche „seit"	32	55
	Die einfache Form und die Verlaufsform des Plusquamperfekts	33	56
L 14	Das Konditional II der Hilfsverben	33	57
	Englische Entsprechungen deutscher modaler Hilfsverben	34	58–62
L 15	Das adjektivische und das substantivische Possessivpronomen	35	63–65
	Das verstärkende *own*	36	66
L 16	Die Verlaufsform des Präsens mit futurischer Bedeutung	37	67
	Das deutsche „man"	37	68
L 17	Verben ohne und mit Objekt	37	69
	Passiv bei Verben mit präpositionalem Objekt	38	70
L 18	Die prädikative Ergänzung zum Subjekt und Objekt	38	71–73
	Das Partizip als prädikative Ergänzung	39	74
	Das deutsche „lassen"	40	75
L 19	Adverbiale Bestimmungen beim Present Perfect	40	76
	Stellung von *so*	41	77
L 20	Die indirekte Rede	41	78
	Die Zeitenfolge in der indirekten Rede	42	79
	Der Fragesatz in der indirekten Rede	43	80
	Der Imperativ in der indirekten Rede	43	81
L 21	Besonderheiten beim Adverb	44	82–84
	Englisches Verb statt deutschem Adverb	45	85
L 22	Der Infinitiv ohne *to* als Teil des direkten Objekts (AcI)	46	86
	Der Infinitiv mit *to* als Teil des direkten Objekts (AcI)	46	87
	Passiver Infinitiv des AcI	47	88
	Der Infinitiv nach passivem Prädikat (NcI)	47	89

Inhalt nach Sachgebieten

§§

Das Substantiv und der Artikel

Das Substantiv (Numerus und Genus) 8–14
Der Plural zusammengesetzter Substantive 8
Substantive, die nur im Plural stehen 9
Substantive, die nur im Singular stehen 10
Verschiedene Bedeutung im Singular und Plural 11
Das Geschlecht der Substantive 12
Singular und Plural bei Zahlenangaben 13
Possessiver Plural 14

Der bestimmte Artikel 48–51
Eigennamen und Zeitbezeichnungen mit und ohne bestimmten Artikel 48
Allgemeinbegriffe mit und ohne bestimmten Artikel 49
Bestimmter Artikel bei näherer Bestimmung 50
Redewendungen mit und ohne bestimmten Artikel 51

Der unbestimmte Artikel 52–53
Nachstellung des unbestimmten Artikels 53

Das Verb

Die unvollständigen Hilfsverben 1–3; 19–20; 57–62; 81
Englische Entsprechungen deutscher modaler Hilfsverben   58–62
Das Konditional II der Hilfsverben 57

Einfache und Verlaufsform 15; 47; 54; 56; 67; 76
Die Verlaufsform des Präsens mit futurischer Bedeutung .. 67
Die einfache und die Verlaufsform des Perfekts 54; 76
Die einfache und die Verlaufsform des Plusquamperfekts   56
Die einfache und die Verlaufsform beim Passiv 15
Verben, die meist keine Verlaufsform bilden 54

Das Passiv 15–18; 68; 70; 88–89
Die einfache und die Verlaufsform beim Passiv 15
Das Passiv bei Verben mit einem und mit zwei Objekten ... 16–17
Das Passiv bei Verben mit präpositionalem Objekt 70
englisch: Passiv – deutsch: ‚man' 18; 68
Der Infinitiv im Passiv 18
Das Partizip Perfekt mit passivem Sinn 45; 75
Passiver Infinitiv des AcI 88
Der Infinitiv nach passivem Prädikat (NcI) 89

Der Infinitiv mit und ohne *to* 18; 20–21; 74–75; 86–89
Der Infinitiv im Passiv 18
Der Infinitiv ohne *to* als Teil des direkten Objekts (AcI) 74; 86
Der Infinitiv mit *to* als Teil des direkten Objekts (AcI) 87
Passiver Infinitiv des AcI 88
Das deutsche ‚lassen' 75; 86
Der Infinitiv nach passivem Prädikat (NcI) 89

	Das Gerundium	40–43; 47
	Das Gerundium im Satzzusammenhang	41
	Das Gerundium nach Präpositionen	42
	Präposition + Gerundium in der Bedeutung eines Nebensatzes	43
	Die Partizipien	44–47; 74–75
	Das Partizip Präsens	44; 46–47; 74
	Das Partizip Perfekt mit passivem Sinn	45; 75
	Das Partizip als prädikative Ergänzung	44; 74
	Das Partizip in der Bedeutung eines Nebensatzes	46
	Die *ing*-Form im Englischen (Überblick)	47
	Die Verbergänzungen	6; 44; 69; 72–74
	Verben ohne Reflexivpronomen	6
	Verben ohne und mit Objekt	69
	Die prädikative Ergänzung zum Subjekt	72; 74
	Die prädikative Ergänzung zum Objekt	73–74
	Das Partizip als prädikative Ergänzung	44; 74
	Die indirekte Rede	78–81
	Die Zeitenfolge in der indirekten Rede	79
	Der Fragesatz in der indirekten Rede	80
	Der Imperativ in der indirekten Rede	81
Das Adjektiv	Adjektive auf -*ly*	82
	Das Adjektiv als Substantiv	22
	Das Adjektiv mit Stützwort	23
	Der Infinitiv mit *to* nach Adjektiven	18; 21
	Das verstärkende *own*	63; 66
Das Adverb	Adjektive auf -*ly* als Adverbien	82
	Adjektiv und Adverb haben dieselbe Form	83
	Adverb mit und ohne -*ly*	84
	Adverbiale Bestimmungen beim Present Perfect	76
	Englisches Verb statt deutschem Adverb	85
Die Pronomen	**Reflexivpronomen**	4–6
	Das Pronomen mit -*self* (Formen und Gebrauch)	4–5
	Verben ohne Reflexivpronomen	6
	Pronomen der Gegenseitigkeit	7
	Relativpronomen und Relativsatz	27–30
	Notwendige und ausmalende Relativsätze	27
	that als Relativpronomen	28
	Der notwendige Relativsatz ohne Relativpronomen	29
	Nachstellung der Präposition im notwendigen Relativsatz ..	30
	Unbestimmte Pronomen	28; 32–38
	all	32
	much, many, a lot of	33
	little, a little – few, a few	34
	no und seine Zusammensetzungen	35

5

	some und *any* und ihre Zusammensetzungen	36
	any in bejahten Sätzen	37
	every – each und ihre Zusammensetzungen	37
	Zusammenfassung der unbestimmten Pronomen	38
	Die Fragepronomen *what* und *which*	39
	Possessivpronomen	14; 63–65
	Das adjektivische Possessivpronomen	64
	Das substantivische Possessivpronomen	65
	Das deutsche ‚man'	17; 68
Präpositionen	Nachstellung der Präposition im Relativ- und Fragesatz	30
	Passiv bei Verben mit präpositionalem Objekt	70
	Das Gerundium nach Präpositionen	42
	Präposition + Gerundium in der Bedeutung eines Nebensatzes	43
	Das deutsche ‚seit' *(since* und *for)*	54–56; 76
Die Frage	Der Infinitiv mit *to* nach Fragewörtern	21
	Die Nachstellung der Präposition beim Fragesatz	30
	Die Fragepronomen *what* und *which*	39
	Der Fragesatz in der indirekten Rede	80
	Kurzfragen	1–2
Zahlen	Singular und Plural bei Zahlenangaben	13
	Der Infinitiv mit *to* nach Ordnungszahlen	21
	Grund- und Ordnungszahlen	25
	Zahlwörter (Wiederholungszahlen; Zahlen der Reihenfolge;	
	Zeitangaben; Gemeine Brüche; Dezimalbrüche)	24
	Maße und Gewichte	26
Wortstellung	Nachstellung der Präposition im Relativ- und Fragesatz	30
	Stellung von *so, nor, neither*	3; 77
	Der Fragesatz in der indirekten Rede	80
Zeichensetzung	Punkt statt Komma bei Dezimalbrüchen	24
	Das Komma	24; 27; 31

1

Kurzfragen (Question Tags) §1

Im gesprochenen Englisch verwendet man oft Kurzfragen, die etwa den deutschen Ausdrücken ‚nicht?', ‚nicht wahr?', ‚oder?' entsprechen, aber viel häufiger gebraucht werden. Diese Kurzfragen nehmen Hilfsverb und Subjekt des vorhergehenden Satzes wieder auf.

1. a) The doors **are** shut, **aren't they?** Die Türen sind doch zu, nicht (wahr)? You **will** be careful, **won't you?** Du bist doch vorsichtig, nicht wahr? Du bist doch hoffentlich vorsichtig? b) The lion **couldn't** break through the window, **could it?** Der Löwe könnte doch wohl nicht ...?	1. a) Ist der Vordersatz bejaht, so ist die Kurzfrage verneint. b) Ist der Vordersatz verneint, so ist die Kurzfrage bejaht.
2. It **sounds** quite close, **doesn't it?** Das klingt doch ganz nahe? You **liked** the film, **didn't you?** Der Film hat dir gefallen, nicht wahr?	2. Ist im Vordersatz kein Hilfsverb vorhanden, so verwendet man in der Kurzfrage eine entsprechende Form von *to do*.

Kurzfrage beim Imperativ (The Imperative with Question Tags) §2

Let's have tea now, **shall we?** Shut the windows, **will you?** Switch the lights on, **will you?**	Wir wollen jetzt Tee trinken, ja? Bitte mach doch die Fenster zu. Mach bitte das Licht an.

Eine Aufforderung klingt höflicher, wenn man an den Imperativ die Kurzfrage *shall we?* oder *will you?* anhängt.

so – nor – neither §3

Dem deutschen ‚ich auch', ‚ich auch nicht' entspricht ein englischer Kurzsatz, der das Hilfsverb des vorhergehenden Satzes wieder aufnimmt. Das Subjekt steht am Satzende.

1. a) "I am glad you didn't shoot King." „Ich bin froh ..." "So am I." „Ich auch." b) "I don't like strong coffee." „Ich mag keinen starken Kaffee." "Nor do I." (oder: "Neither do I.") „Ich auch nicht." I couldn't help you. Ich konnte ... Nor could Doris. Doris auch nicht.	1. a) Ist der Vordersatz bejaht, dann beginnt der Kurzsatz mit *so*. b) Ist der Vordersatz verneint, dann beginnt der Kurzsatz mit *nor* (oder: *neither*).

2. "I think we have deserved the tickets after that shock." „Ich glaube, wir haben..." "So do I, sir." „Das meine ich auch."	2. Ist im Vordersatz kein Hilfsverb vorhanden, dann verwendet man im Kurzsatz eine entsprechende Form von *to do*.

Beachte: In der Umgangssprache wird statt *neither* die Form *not either* bevorzugt:
"I don't like that weather." – "I don't either."

2

Das Pronomen mit '-self' (The Pronoun with '-self')

Formen § 4

Infinitiv: to defend oneself sich verteidigen	
I defend **myself** [mai'self] mich (selbst) you defend **yourself** dich (selbst) he defends **himself** she defends **herself** } sich (selbst) it defends **itself**	we defend **ourselves** [vz] uns (selbst) you defend **yourselves** euch (selbst) they defend **themselves** sich (selbst)

Gebrauch: Das Pronomen mit *-self* dient § 5

1. I saw **the Queen herself.** Ich sah die Königin selbst. **I myself** saw the Queen. } Ich selbst... I saw the Queen **myself.**	1. zur Hervorhebung von Substantiven und Pronomen. In diesem Fall ist es stark betont.
2. I said to **myself**... Jack bought **himself** a book. We found **ourselves** on a bus.	2. als Objekt, wenn dieses dieselbe Person ist wie das Subjekt. In diesem Fall ist es nicht betont.

Vergleiche: Tom bought **him** (his friend) a book. Tom kaufte ihm...
Tom bought **himself** (Tom) a book. Tom kaufte sich...

Englische Verben ohne Reflexivpronomen § 6

Vielen englischen Verben oder verbalen Ausdrücken ohne Reflexivpronomen entsprechen deutsche Verben mit Reflexivpronomen:

to be afraid of	sich fürchten vor	to fancy	sich vorstellen
to be angry	sich ärgern	to feel (well)	sich (wohl)fühlen
to be glad	sich freuen	to get ready	sich fertigmachen
to be late	sich verspäten	to happen	sich ereignen
to catch a cold	sich erkälten	to hurry	sich beeilen

to lie down	sich hinlegen	to remember	sich erinnern an
to meet	sich treffen	to sit down	sich setzen
to move	sich bewegen	to turn round	sich umdrehen
to open	sich öffnen	to wonder	sich fragen
to part	sich trennen	to worry	sich Sorgen machen

closed
Beachte: Manche Verben können mit oder ohne Reflexivpronomen verwendet werden:
to dress, to dress oneself — sich anziehen
to wash, to wash oneself — sich waschen

Pronomen der Gegenseitigkeit (Reciprocal Pronouns) § 7
each other — one another

Im Deutschen wird das Reflexivpronomen (sich, uns, euch) auch zum Ausdruck der Gegenseitigkeit verwendet: Die Kinder halfen sich = Die Kinder halfen einander (gegenseitig). Im Englischen muß man in diesem Falle *each other* oder *one another* gebrauchen.

Colin and Diana took photographs of **each other**.	Colin und Diana photographierten sich (gegenseitig).
The boys and the girls helped **one another**.	Die Jungen und Mädchen halfen sich (gegenseitig).
We told **one another** our adventures.	Wir erzählten uns (einer dem anderen) unsere Abenteuer.

Vergleiche:
He saw himself in the mirror. — Er sah sich im Spiegel.
They saw each other for the first time. — Sie sahen sich zum ersten Mal.

3

introduce = bekannt machen

Das Substantiv (Numerus und Genus) (The Noun)
Der Plural zusammengesetzter Substantive § 8
(The Plural of Compound Nouns)

1. boy **scouts** apple-**trees** passers-by sisters-in-law lookers-on	motor-**cars** motor-**cycles** home**towns** picture **postcards** market-**places**	1. Ist das Grundwort ein Substantiv, so erhält dieses das Plural-s.
2. good-for-**nothings** grown-**ups**		2. Ist kein substantivisches Grundwort vorhanden, so tritt das Plural-s an das letzte Wort.

Substantive, die nur im Plural stehen § 9
(Nouns Used only in the Plural)

Immer im Plural stehen:

1. clothes	Kleidung	2. scales	Waage
goods	Waren	scissors	Schere
stairs	Treppe	spectacles	Brille
surroundings	Umgebung	glasses	
contents	Inhalt	shorts	kurze Hose
		trousers	(lange) Hose
		pyjamas	Schlafanzug

Beachte zu 2.: Nach dem unbestimmten Artikel und nach Zahlenangaben gebraucht man *pair of:* a pair of scissors eine Schere; two pairs of scissors zwei Scheren

Substantive, die nur im Singular stehen § 10
(Nouns Used only in the Singular)

Your **advice** was good.	Immer im Singular stehen einige Allgemeinbegriffe und Sammelnamen wie	
Ihre Ratschläge waren gut.		
The girls want to improve their **knowledge** of English.	advice	Ratschlag, Ratschläge
	business	Geschäft(e)
... ihre Englischkenntnisse ...	information	Auskunft, Auskünfte
I have made good **progress** in English.	knowledge	Kenntnis(se)
... gute Fortschritte ...	progress	Fortschritt(e)
The **furniture** of the house was lovely.	news	Nachricht(en)
Die Möbel ... waren ...	furniture	Möbel

Beachte: 1. He gave me a good piece of advice.   ... einen guten Rat.
          You gave me a good piece of information.   ... eine gute Auskunft.
          an interesting piece of news   eine interessante Nachricht
          a fine piece of furniture   ein schönes Möbelstück
    2. *USA (United States of America)* wird oft wie ein Singular gebraucht:
       The USA is a big country.   Die Vereinigten Staaten sind ein großes Land.

Verschiedene Bedeutung im Singular und Plural § 11
(Different Meaning in the Singular and in the Plural)

Gesamtvorstellung	Einzelvorstellung
a) **Tea** is good for you.	b) Our grocer has good **teas**. Teesorten
Do you like English **food**?	Some **foods** are cheaper in England than in Germany. Lebensmittel
I like **coffee**.	Two more **coffees**? Tassen Kaffee

Sammel- und Stoffnamen stehen
a) im Singular (ohne den bestimmten Artikel), b) im Plural, wenn mehrere Einzelstücke
   wenn der Gesamtbegriff gemeint ist: oder verschiedenartige Sorten gemeint
                                            sind:

fish	Fisch, Fische	fishes	Fischarten, einzelne Fische
fruit	Obst, Früchte	fruits	Obstsorten
food	Nahrung	foods	verschiedene Lebensmittel
hair	Haar, Haare	hairs	(einzelne) Haare
coffee	Kaffee	coffees	(Tassen oder Sorten) Kaffee
tea	Tee	teas	Teesorten

Beachte: 1. people = ‚Leute' hat nie ein Plural-s:
Many people were in the street.   Viele Leute waren auf der Straße.
2. police = ‚Polizei' wird wie ein Plural gebraucht:
The police are very busy.   Die Polizei ist sehr beschäftigt.

Das Geschlecht der Substantive (The Gender of Nouns) § 12

Das natürliche Geschlecht bei Personen und Tieren wird unterschieden durch:

Personen		Tiere		
man	– woman	cock	– hen	1. verschiedene Bezeichnungen für männliches und weibliches Geschlecht
gentleman	– lady	bull, ox	– cow	
boy	– girl	gander	– goose	
husband	– wife			
boy-friend	– girl-friend	he-bear	– she-bear	2. Zusatzwörter
male nurse	– nurse	male wolf	– female wolf	
teacher	– woman teacher	tom-cat	– she-cat	
male worker	– female worker	bull elephant	– cow elephant	
steward	– stewardess	lion	– lioness	3. die Endung -ess bei weiblichen Lebewesen
waiter	– waitress	tiger	– tigress	
host	– hostess			
prince	– princess			

Beachte: 1. Ergibt sich das Geschlecht aus dem Zusammenhang, so braucht es nicht gekennzeichnet zu werden:
Bob went to school with his **friend Jane**.
2. Ist das natürliche Geschlecht eines Tieres bekannt, so kann man das entsprechende Pronomen verwenden:
The dog runs after **his** master.
Besitzt das Tier einen Rufnamen, so treten *he* oder *she* an die Stelle von *it*.
3. Weiblich werden oft Fahrzeuge und Ländernamen gebraucht:
Our car is 10 years old and **she** still runs well.
The 'Queen Mary' and **her** sister-ship ...
Britain builds most of **her** ships **herself**.

Singular und Plural bei Zahlenangaben § 13
(Singular and Plural with Numbers)

three pounds ten shillings = three **pound** ten five feet two inches = five **foot** two	*Pound* und *foot* stehen oft im Singular, wenn eine kleinere unbenannte Maßeinheit folgt.

Beachte den Singular bei Ausdrücken wie:
a sixty-**minute** journey; a nine-**year**-old boy; a three-**mile** walk; a ten-**shilling** note.

Possessiver Plural (German Singular – English Plural) § 14

Bezeichnungen für Körperteile oder Kleidungsstücke stehen im Plural, wenn von mehreren Personen die Rede ist. Im Deutschen steht hier meist der Singular:

They shook their **heads**. We took off our **coats**.	Sie schüttelten den Kopf. Wir zogen den Mantel aus.

Merke auch: Many people lost their **lives**.   Viele Menschen verloren das Leben.
Many English houses have **gardens**.   Viele englische Häuser haben einen Garten.
They made up their **minds** . . .   Sie faßten den Entschluß . . .

4

Das Passiv: einfache Form und Verlaufsform § 15
(The Passive Voice: Ordinary and Continuous Form)

Einfache Form: Zustand – Vorgang	Verlaufsform: Vorgang
The house is built. . . . ist gebaut, . . . wird gebaut The house was built. . . . war gebaut, . . . wurde gebaut The house has been built. The house had been built. The house will be built. The house would be built.	The house is being built. . . . wird (gerade) gebaut The house was being built. . . . wurde (gerade) gebaut

Die einfache Form des Passivs gibt es **in allen Zeiten.**

Sie bezeichnet entweder einen Zustand oder einen Vorgang.

Die Verlaufsform des Passivs gibt es **nur im Präsens und im Präteritum.** Sie wird mit *to be being* gebildet. Man verwendet sie, wenn eindeutig ein Vorgang bezeichnet werden soll, **der begonnen hat, aber noch nicht zu Ende ist.**

Der Passivsatz (The Passive Voice in the Sentence)

1. bei Verben mit einem Objekt   § 16

S	P	O	
a) A man	approached	Mike.	a) Das Objekt des Aktivsatzes wird zum Subjekt des Passivsatzes.
Mike	was approached	by a man.	
b) Mike	helped	the police.	b) Dabei spielt es keine Rolle, ob es sich im deutschen Satz um ein Dativ- oder um ein Akkusativobjekt handelt.
The police	were helped	by Mike.	

Englische Verben mit direktem Objekt

Im Gegensatz zu den entsprechenden deutschen Verben haben die folgenden englischen Verben ein direktes Objekt und bilden ein persönliches Passiv:

to answer s.o.	jdm. antworten	to join s.o.	sich jdm. anschließen
to approach s.o.	sich jdm. nähern	to meet s.o.	jdm. begegnen
to follow s.o.	jdm. folgen	to remember s.o.	sich an jdn. erinnern
to forgive s.o.	jdm. vergeben	to thank s.o.	jdm. danken
to help s.o.	jdm. helfen	to trust s.o.	jdm. vertrauen

2. bei Verben mit zwei Objekten   § 17

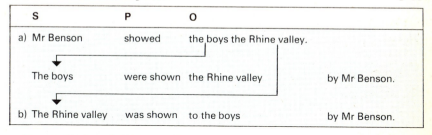

a) Hat ein Verb zwei Objekte (Dativ- und Akkusativobjekt – indirektes und direktes Objekt), so wird meist das Dativobjekt zum Subjekt des Passivsatzes.
b) Auch das Akkusativobjekt kann gelegentlich zum Subjekt des Passivsatzes werden.

Verben mit zwei Objekten

| to bring | to hand | to offer | to pay | to sell | to show |
| to give | to leave | to pass | to promise | to send | to tell |

Beachte: englisch: Passiv   deutsch: „man"
        Mike was shown the contents.   Man zeigte Mike den Inhalt.
        I was given two pound notes.   Man gab mir zwei Pfundnoten.

Der Infinitiv im Passiv (The Passive Infinitive) § 18

Infinitiv Aktiv:

to call	rufen	— to have called	gerufen haben
to see	sehen	— to have seen	gesehen haben

Infinitiv Passiv:

to be called	gerufen werden	— to have been called	gerufen worden sein
to be seen	gesehen werden	— to have been seen	gesehen worden sein

Einem passiven Infinitiv, besonders nach *to be* und *to remain*, entspricht oft ein deutscher aktiver Infinitiv.

The book **is to be had.**	Das Buch ist zu haben.
	(= kann gekauft werden.)
Friends and relations **were to be seen.**	Freunde und Verwandte waren zu sehen.
	(= konnten gesehen werden.)
There is a lot of work **to be done.**	Viel Arbeit ist (bleibt) zu tun.
Much work **remains to be done.**	(= muß, soll getan werden.)

Beachte: Nach Adjektiven steht kein Passiv:
    This text is **easy to translate.**   Dieser Text ist leicht zu übersetzen.
    This poem is **hard to understand.**   Dieses Gedicht ist schwer zu verstehen.
    Is English **difficult to learn?**   Ist Englisch schwer zu lernen?

5

Die unvollständigen Hilfsverben und ihre Ersatzverben § 19
(The Defective Auxiliaries and their Substitutes)
(vgl. Grammatisches Beiheft zu A 1 neu § 64)

Unvollständige Hilfsverben haben keinen Infinitiv, kein -s in der 3. Person und können nicht alle Zeiten bilden. Für die fehlenden Zeiten treten Ersatzverben mit ähnlicher Bedeutung ein.

Präsens	Verneinte Form	Präteritum/Konditional	Ersatzverb
I can	**I cannot, can't**	**I could**	**to be able to**
ich kann		a) ich konnte	
(Fähigkeit)		b) ich könnte	

1. **Can** you speak English? – 2. No, I **cannot.**
3. a) I **couldn't** find my pen.
   b) **Could** you help me?
4. I **shall be able to** go to England.

Präsens	Verneinte Form	Konditional	Ersatzverb
I may a) ich darf b) ich kann (vielleicht)	**I may not** ich darf nicht	**I might** a) ich dürfte b) ich könnte	a) **to be allowed to**

1. a) **May** I go home now? – 2. No, you **may not**.
1. b) You **may** be right, but we shall try nevertheless.
3. b) You **might** get a different seat when you come back.
4. **Were you allowed to** stay and watch the fire?

Präsens	Verneinte Form	Konditional	Ersatzverben
I must ich muß	**I mustn't** ich darf nicht **I needn't** ich brauche nicht	Ersatzverb: **I should have to** ich müßte	**to have to** **to have got to** **not to be allowed to**

1. **Must** I go soon? – 2. No, you **needn't**.
3. If I hadn't done my homework yesterday I **should have to** do it today.
4. You **have got to** leave the cinema.

Präsens	Konditional
shall I? soll ich?	**you, he should** du, er sollte(st) **he ought to** er sollte eigentlich

1. **Shall** I go now?
2. They **shouldn't** blame you. – They **ought to** know that the law must be respected.

Präsens	Verneinte Form	Präteritum/Konditional	Ersatzverben
will you? willst du? ... bitte Yes, **I will.**	**won't you?** willst du nicht?	a) **he would not** er wollte nicht b) **would you?** würden Sie?	**to want to** **to wish to**

1. Please hurry, **will you?**
2. **Won't you** come tomorrow?
3. a) The cat **would not** stay in the house.
   b) **Would you** please shut the door?
4. I **wanted to** shout a warning and rush outside.

Beachte: 1. Das Präteritum zu *I can* heißt *I could* oder *I was able to*.
2. ‚Ich kann Englisch' heißt *I know English* oder *I can speak English*.
3. Für ‚wollen' wird im Präsens fast immer das Ersatzverb *to want to* verwendet.

Der Infinitiv ohne 'to' (The Infinitive without 'to') § 20

Der Infinitiv ohne *to* steht

1. **I cannot see** him. **I must go** now.	1. nach den Hilfsverben (außer *ought to*, vgl. § 19)
2. **I had better keep** quiet. Es wäre besser, wenn ich . . . **I would rather stay** here. Ich würde, möchte lieber . . .	2. nach einigen Redewendungen, z. B. *I had better, I would rather*

Der Infinitiv mit 'to' (The Infinitive with 'to') § 21

Der Infinitiv mit *to* steht

1. a) It is **the first** fire drill **to take place** in this house. . . . die in diesem Hause stattfindet. b) The first rows will be **the last to leave**. . . . die hinausgehen. c) **The best thing to do** is to keep quiet. Das beste, was man tun kann...	1. an Stelle eines deutschen Relativsatzes a) nach Ordnungszahlen: *the first, the second, the third,* etc. b) nach *the last* c) nach Superlativen
2. I did not **know what to think** of it. (= I did not know what I should think of it.) . . . was ich davon halten sollte. **I wondered whether to stay or to leave.** . . . ob ich bleiben oder weggehen sollte.	2. an Stelle eines indirekten Fragesatzes in Verbindung mit einem Fragewort *(how to, where to, what to, whether to)* nach einer Reihe von Verben: to ask to remember to tell to forget to see to understand to know to show to wonder to learn to teach

Beachte: In der Umgangssprache steht nach *to come, to go* und *to try* oft der Infinitiv mit *and:* I'll **try and find** a better place for the tent.

6

Das Adjektiv als Substantiv (The Adjective used as a Noun) § 22

Ein Adjektiv kann mit dem bestimmten Artikel auch als Substantiv verwendet werden. Es bezeichnet dann

1. the good
    the poor
    the dead
	die Guten
	die Armen
	die Toten
		1. eine Gesamtheit von Personen
		    (ohne Plural-s)

2. the good
  the impossible
  the beautiful
	das Gute
	das Unmögliche
	das Schöne
		2. einen allgemeinen Begriff

Beachte: Einige Adjektive sind wirkliche Substantive (mit Plural-s) geworden:
the whites and the blacks   die Weißen und die Schwarzen

Das Adjektiv mit Stützwort (The Adjective with Prop-word) § 23

1. a dead man
  a poor woman
  a sick person
  a good thing
  the little ones
	ein Toter
	eine Arme
	ein Kranker
	etwas Gutes
	die Kleinen
		1. Soll ein alleinstehendes Adjektiv
		nicht eine Gesamtheit, sondern ein
		oder mehrere einzelne bezeichnen,
		so wird ihm ein Stützwort beigegeben,
		z. B. *man, woman, person, thing, one.*

2. Claudius took thousands of prisoners, **the old ones** were given their freedom, **the young ones** were sent to Rome as slaves. ... die alten ... die jungen		2. Soll ein vorhergenanntes Substantiv nicht wiederholt werden, so tritt hinter das Adjektiv an seine Stelle das Stützwort *one, ones.*

Beachte: 1. Which boy did you see, **this one** or **that one?** ... den hier oder den dort?
 2. Das Stützwort *one, ones* steht jedoch nicht nach Superlativen mit bestimmtem Artikel:
  Of all the British chiefs Caractacus was **the bravest.**
 3. Ordnungszahlen werden meist ohne Stützwort gebraucht:
  Have you ever had a car before? Yes, this is **our second.**

Zahlwörter (Numerals) § 24

1. Wiederholungszahlen		2. Zahlen der Reihenfolge	
once	einmal	firstly	erstens
twice	zweimal	secondly	zweitens
three times	dreimal	thirdly	drittens
four times	viermal	in the fourth place	viertens
five times	fünfmal	in the fifth place	fünftens
six times	sechsmal	in the sixth place	sechstens
seven times	siebenmal	in the seventh place	siebtens
eight times	achtmal	in the eighth place	achtens
etc.	etc.	etc.	etc.

3. Zeitangaben			
a week	8 Tage	6 months	ein halbes Jahr
a fortnight	14 Tage	9 months	ein Dreivierteljahr
3 months	ein Vierteljahr	18 months	anderthalb Jahre

4. Gemeine Brüche

½	a (one) half		⅔ mile	two thirds of a mile
⅓	a (one) third		½ mile	aber: half a mile
¼	a (one) quarter		3¾ miles	three miles and three
⅕	a (one) fifth			quarters
⅐	a (one) seventh			three and three quarter
¹/₂₅	a (one) twenty-fifth			miles
⅗	three fifths		2½ lbs.	two pounds and a half
⅝	five eighths			two and a half pounds
1¾	one and three quarters			
6⁷/₁₂	six and seven twelfths			
25⁹/₁₀	twenty-five and nine tenths			

5. Dezimalbrüche

56.19 fifty-six point one nine = deutsch: 56,19
7.08 seven point nought eight = deutsch: 7,08
.73 point seven three = deutsch: 0,73

Beachte: Statt Komma steht Punkt *(decimal point)*. Vor dem Punkt bleibt 0 weg.

Grund- und Ordnungszahlen (Cardinal and Ordinal Numbers) § 25

Grundzahlen	Ordnungszahlen
101 a hundred and one one hundred and one	101st the hundred and first
159 a hundred and fifty-nine one hundred and fifty-nine	159th the hundred and fifty-ninth
200 two hundred	200th the two hundredth
300 three hundred	300th the three hundredth
1,000 a (one) thousand	1,000th the thousandth
2,000 two thousand	2,000th the two thousandth
4,810 four thousand eight hundred and ten	4,810th the four thousand eight hundred and tenth
1,000,000 a (one) million [ˈmiljən]	1,000,000th the millionth
2,000,000 two million	2,000,000th the two millionth

Beachte: 1. Zehner und Einer werden an *hundred* oder *thousand* durch *and* angeschlossen.
2. Nach Tausendern steht immer ein Komma: *30,000.*
3. *Hundred, thousand* und *million* erhalten nur dann in der Mehrzahl ein -s, wenn sie als Hauptwörter gebraucht sind:
three hundred children aber: hundreds of children
three thousand years thousands of years
four million pounds millions of pounds
4. Bei Jahreszahlen steht immer *in* . . ., selten *in the year* . . .
in 1952 = in nineteen (hundred and) fifty-two; in 1066 = in ten sixty-six

Maße und Gewichte (Measures and Weights) § 26

Bezeichnung			Abkürzung	entspricht	
inch [intʃ]		Zoll	in., ins.		2,54 cm
foot [fut]		Fuß	ft.	12 inches	30,5 cm
yard [jɑːd]		Yard	yd., yds.	3 feet	91,5 cm
mile [mail]		Meile	m.	1,760 yards	1,6 km
ounce [auns]		Unze	oz.		28 g
pound [paund]		Pfund	lb., lbs.	16 ounces	454 g
hundredweight *(engl.)* ['hʌndrədweit]	}	Zentner	cwt.	112 pounds	51 kg
hundredweight *(am.)*			cwt.	100 pounds	45 kg
ton [tʌn] *(engl.)*	}	Tonne	tn.	2 240 pounds	1 016 kg
ton *(am.)*			tn.	2 000 pounds	907 kg

7

Der Relativsatz (The Relative Clause)

Notwendige und ausmalende Relativsätze § 27
(Defining and Non-defining Relative Clauses)

1. People **who drive too fast** should be punished.	1. Der **notwendige** Relativsatz gibt eine genaue Bestimmung des Wortes, auf das er sich bezieht. Er ist zum Verständnis des Satzes **unentbehrlich**.
2. My brother Jack, **who is 18 years old,** has bought a bicycle.	2. Der **ausmalende** Relativsatz ist ein Zusatz. Er ist zum Verständnis des Satzes **entbehrlich**.

Beachte: Notwendige Relativsätze werden beim Sprechen ohne Pause an den Hauptsatz angeschlossen und beim Schreiben nicht durch Komma von diesem getrennt.

'That' als Relativpronomen (The Relative Pronoun 'that') § 28

'That' als Relativpronomen steht im notwendigen Relativsatz

1. Nobody knew of **the terrible danger that** was waiting for them. Beowulf locked his arms round **the creature that** no weapon could hurt.	1. meist bei Sachen, seltener bei Personen

2. **Everything that** was shown was interesting. Alles, was . . . There was **nothing that** could be done against Grendel. . . . nichts, was . . .	2. immer nach *all* (alles, was), *everything, something, anything, nothing, much, little*
3. Grendel was **the most dangerous monster that** lived in Denmark. Beowulf was not **the first person that** wanted to destroy the monster. He was **the only man that** overpowered Grendel.	3. meist nach Superlativen und nach *the first*, *the last*, *the only*

Der notwendige Relativsatz ohne Relativpronomen   § 29
(The Defining Relative Clause without a Relative Pronoun)

O S P	
The apple (that/which) I found was bad. The man (that/whom) we saw was our baker.	Das Pronomen des notwendigen Relativsatzes kann wegbleiben, wenn es Objekt des Relativsatzes ist.

Beachte: Das Relativpronomen kann nicht ausgelassen werden, wenn es Subjekt des Relativsatzes ist:
Where are the books **that** were lying on this table yesterday?

Die Nachstellung der Präposition   § 30
(The Preposition in the End Position)

1. That was the moment **(that)** Grendel had waited **for**. Grendel felt the danger **(that)** he was **in**.	1. Im notwendigen Relativsatz steht die Präposition oft nicht am Satzanfang, sondern hinter dem Verb.
2. Where do you come **from**? Woher? What are you looking **for**? Wonach? What do you want this knife **for**? Wofür? Wozu?	2. Im Fragesatz steht eine zum Verb gehörende Präposition am Satzende.

Beachte: 1. Bei *where?* = ‚wohin?' steht gelegentlich die Präposition *to*:
    Where are you going **(to)**?
    2. In der Umgangssprache wird die Form *whom* nicht verwendet. Statt dessen steht *who*:
    Who is this letter written **to**? Who are you waiting **for**?

Das Komma (The Comma) § 31

Abweichend vom Deutschen steht

1. a) He, therefore, wished to see his uncle. My father, however, did not like it. b) Mr Benson said, "Let us go." c) Dear Uncle Jack, ...	1. **ein Komma** a) bei eingeschobenen adverbialen Bestimmungen, besonders auch bei *therefore* und *however* b) oft vor der wörtlichen Rede statt des seltenen Doppelpunktes c) nach der Anrede im Brief
2. a) The little boy I played with is my brother. b) He hoped to be back in an hour. c) Look before you cross the street. I wonder whether I shall see him tomorrow.	2. **kein Komma** a) vor und nach notwendigen Relativsätzen b) vor Infinitivsätzen c) meist vor nachgestellten Nebensätzen mit Konjunktion

8

Einige unbestimmte Pronomen (Some Indefinite Pronouns)

all § 32

1. He lost **all faith**. ... den ganzen Glauben. He slept **all the time**. ... die ganze Zeit	1. all + Singular = ganz
2. **All children** like ice-cream. Alle Kinder ... **All the four children** rushed into the clear water. Alle vier Kinder ...	2. all + Plural = alle

much, many, a lot of § 33

1. I haven't **much** time. ... nicht viel Zeit. Do you read **much**? Liest du viel? **How much** will you pay for that job? Wieviel ...?	1. much = viel

2. I haven't **many** friends. ...nicht viele Freunde. Did you see **many** things? ...viele Dinge (vieles)...? **How many** people were hurt in that accident? Wie viele Menschen...?	2. many = viele

Beachte: 1. *Much* und *many* haben dieselben Steigerungsformen: *more, most*.
          I have **more money** than you have.   Ich habe mehr Geld als du.
          Most English houses have open fires.   Die meisten englischen Häuser...
      2. In bejahten Sätzen gebraucht man nicht *much / many*, sondern fast immer
        a lot (lots) of, plenty of, a great number of.
        There is **a lot of work** to do.   ...viel Arbeit
        There is **plenty of time** to go to the station.   ...viel Zeit
        A great number of years passed by.   Viele Jahre...

little, a little – few, a few   § 34

1. I have **little** money. ...wenig Geld. He has still **a little** time. ...noch ein wenig Zeit.	1. little + Singular = wenig a little + Singular = ein wenig
2. He has **few** friends. ...wenige Freunde. He gave me **a few** apples. ...ein paar Äpfel.	2. few + Plural = wenige a few + Plural = einige, ein paar

Beachte die Steigerungsformen: little – less – least; few – fewer – fewest.

'No' und seine Zusammensetzungen ('No' and its Compounds)   § 35

The beggar had **no** money. Der Bettler hatte kein Geld. **Nobody (no one)** recognized Robin Hood. Niemand erkannte Robin Hood. The poor pedlar had **nothing** to eat. ...hatte nichts zu essen. We could find it **nowhere**. Wir konnten es nirgends finden. I want to buy a skirt, but there is **none** that fits me. ...keiner, der mir paßt. **None** of my friends could help me. Keiner meiner Freunde konnte mir helfen.	no = kein nobody no one } = niemand, keiner nothing = nichts nowhere = nirgends, nirgendwo(hin) none = keiner,e,es (nur mit Bezug auf ein vorangehendes oder folgendes Substantiv)

10

Die Partizipien (The Participles)

Formen:

Präsens Aktiv: helping
Perfekt Aktiv: having helped

Präsens Passiv: (being) helped
Perfekt Passiv: (having been) helped

Anwendung:

1. **Das Partizip Präsens** *(Present Participle)* steht §44

a) John **sat** there **looking** round. J. saß da und schaute sich um. Like a whirlwind he **came sweeping** down the Thames Valley. Wie ein Wirbelwind kam er das Themsetal heruntergefegt. We **stood watching** the people. Wir standen und beobachteten die Leute.	a) nach Verben der Ruhe und Bewegung: to come to run to go to sit to lie to stand to remain to stay
b) They could **see the royal banner flying** in the wind. Sie konnten die königliche Fahne im Wind flattern sehen. We **heard the men talking** to each other. Wir hörten die Männer miteinander sprechen. I **noticed a small car passing** over the bridge. Ich bemerkte, wie ein kleines Auto über die Brücke fuhr.	b) nach Verben der Wahrnehmung: to feel to hear to notice to see to watch

2. **Das Partizip Perfekt** *(Past Participle)* steht mit passivem Sinn §45

a) John **had** men **thrown** into prison without a fair trial. John ließ Menschen ins Gefängnis werfen… Mr Brown **has** his car **washed.** Mr Brown läßt seinen Wagen waschen. I **got** my hair **cut.** Ich ließ mir die Haare schneiden.	a) nach to have } to get } + Akkusativ (dt. lassen = veranlassen)
b) I **heard** my name **shouted.** Ich hörte meinen Namen rufen. …, wie mein Name gerufen wurde. I **felt** my arm **touched.** Ich fühlte, wie mich jemand am Arm berührte.	b) nach Verben der Wahrnehmung

Das Partizip in der Bedeutung eines Nebensatzes § 46

Das Partizip wird im Deutschen oft durch einen Nebensatz wiedergegeben, und zwar

1. He gave me **a letter written** by his mother. ..., der ... geschrieben war. John did not keep **the promises given** in Magna Carta. ..., die er ... gegeben hatte.	1. durch einen Relativsatz
2. He made the barons angry, **taking** their land away and **forcing** them to pay large sums of money to him. ..., indem er ihr Land wegnahm und sie zwang, ...	2. durch einen Nebensatz der Art und Weise
3. **Seeing a policeman,** I quickly went up to him. Als ich einen Polizisten sah, ... **The weather being fine,** they made good progress. Da das Wetter schön war, ...	3. durch einen Nebensatz der Zeit und des Grundes

Beachte: Manchmal ist eine Konjunktion notwendig, um den Sinn der Partizipialkonstruktion zu verdeutlichen:

When mounting the throne of England, Henry III confirmed the Great Charter.
Als er den Thron von England bestieg, ...
He even managed to smile, **as if delighted** to meet so many of his barons.
..., als ob er erfreut wäre, ...

Die ing-Form im Englischen (Überblick) § 47

Bildung: to read — reading; to write — writing; to swim — swimming

Anwendung:

1. Present Participle

verbal (mit Objekt): I saw him writing a letter.   Ich sah ihn, wie er ...
adjektivisch: an interesting book   ein interessantes Buch

2. Continuous Form (in allen Zeiten des Aktivs und im Präsens und Präteritum des Passivs)

I am writing a letter.   Ich schreibe (gerade) ...
We were writing a letter.   Wir schrieben (gerade) ...
The house is being built.   Das Haus wird (gerade) gebaut.

3. Gerund

verbal (mit Objekt): Making dresses is her hobby.   Kleider zu nähen ...
substantivisch: The making of dresses is her hobby.   (Das) Kleidernähen ist ...

'Some' und 'any' und ihre Zusammensetzungen § 36
('Some' and 'any' and their Compounds)

1. a) Here is **some** tea for you. ... (etwas) Tee ... There are **some** mistakes in that letter. ... einige (ein paar) Fehler ... **Some** houses have open fires. Manche Häuser ... b) May I have **some** more tea, please? ... noch (etwas) Tee ...	1. *some* steht a) im bejahten Satz b) in einer höflichen Bitte
2. a) We haven't **any** bread in the house. ... kein Brot ... b) If there are still **any** questions, please say so. Falls es noch (irgendwelche) Fragen gibt, ... c) Are there **any** letters for me? Sind Briefe für mich da?	2. *any* steht a) im verneinten Satz b) im Bedingungssatz c) im Fragesatz (oft unübersetzt)

Some und *any* bezeichnen
1. im Singular eine unbestimmte Menge – dt. ‚etwas' (oder unübersetzt)
2. im Plural eine unbestimmte Anzahl
    some = einige, ein paar, manche (oder unübersetzt)
    any   = irgendwelche (oder unübersetzt)

Zusammensetzungen:

something	etwas	anything	irgend etwas
somebody someone	} jemand	anybody anyone	} irgend jemand
somewhere	irgendwo(hin)	anywhere	irgendwo(hin)
somehow	irgendwie		
sometimes	manchmal		

Beachte:
not ... any	= no	kein	
not ... anybody not ... anyone	= nobody = no one	} niemand	
not ... anything	= nothing	nichts	
not ... anywhere	= nowhere	nirgends, nirgendwo(hin)	

every – each § 37

1. **Every house** has a kitchen. He comes **every day**. (= Monday and Tuesday and Wednesday, etc.)	1. every = jeder, e, es ohne Ausnahme

2. **Each boy of our group** is a boy scout. These books cost two shillings **each**. Diese Bücher kosten je ... We had two cups of coffee **each**. Wir tranken jeder zwei Tassen Kaffee.	2. each = jeder einzelne aus einer begrenzten Anzahl

Beachte: *Any* in bejahten Sätzen = jeder beliebige; irgendein
He may come **any** day. (Monday or Tuesday or Wednesday, etc.)
She would have done **anything**. Sie würde alles (alles Erdenkliche) getan haben.

Zusammensetzungen: everyone ⎫
                                everybody ⎬ jeder, alle   everywhere überall
                                everything ⎭   each one   jeder einzelne
                                                   alles

Unbestimmte Pronomen (Zusammenfassung)   § 38

Plural: Anzahl (zählbar)	**Singular:** Menge (nicht zählbar)
○ ○	BUTTER
Gesamtheit all (the) apples alle Äpfel	**all the butter** die ganze Butter
Große Anzahl many apples viele Äpfel dafür oft: a lot of apples	**Große Menge** much butter viel Butter dafür fast immer: a lot of butter
Kleine Anzahl few apples wenige Äpfel a few apples einige (ein paar) Äpfel	**Kleine Menge** little butter wenig Butter a little butter ein wenig (bißchen) Butter
Unbestimmte Anzahl some apples einige (ein paar) Äpfel ... any apples? (irgendwelche) Äpfel?	**Unbestimmte Menge** some butter etwas Butter ... any butter? (etwas) Butter?
Nicht vorhandene Anzahl no apples ⎫ not ... any apples ⎬ keine Äpfel	**Nicht vorhandene Menge** no butter ⎫ not ... any butter ⎬ keine Butter

Beachte: Das Gegenteil von *many, more, most* ist *few, fewer, fewest*;
               das Gegenteil von *much, more, most* ist *little, less, least*.

what – which   § 39

What books have you read? **What famous men** do you know? **What countries** do you know?	**Which of these books** belong(s) to you? **Which of them** are still living? **Which European countries** have you visited?

Mit *which* fragt man nach Personen oder Sachen aus einer begrenzten Anzahl.

9

Das Gerundium (The Gerund) § 40

Form: Das Gerundium entspricht in der Form dem Partizip Präsens:
to read – reading;   to write – writing;   to swim – swimming

Das Gerundium ist eine Verbform, die als Substantiv verwendet wird. Wie ein Verb kann es aber ein Objekt bei sich haben:
Collecting stamps is an interesting hobby. **Learning English** is not easy.

Es kann aber auch wie ein gewöhnliches Substantiv den bestimmten Artikel und einen of-Genitiv bei sich haben:
The collecting of stamps is an interesting hobby. He liked **the collecting of stamps**.

Im Deutschen kann man in vielen Fällen das Gerundium entweder substantivisch oder verbal, d. h. mit einem Infinitiv, wiedergeben:
The collecting of stamps is a nice hobby. (Das) **Briefmarkensammeln** ist ein schönes Hobby.
Briefmarken zu sammeln ist ein schönes Hobby.

Das Gerundium im Satzzusammenhang (The Gerund in the Sentence)

Das Gerundium steht § 41

1. **Fighting** was soon to be expected. Most of **the crossing** was made in the night. There was a lot of **coming and going**. It was no use **attacking** the English on the hill.	1. als Subjekt, besonders nach: there is there was it is no good $\}$ es hat keinen Zweck it is no use
2. The teacher **began reading**. Boys **like playing** football. Mike **prefers playing** cricket.	2. **häufig** nach folgenden Verben: to begin to love to continue to prefer to hate to start to like
3. He **could not help feeling** sad. The Normans **kept on storming** up the hill. The bravest men of England had **stopped fighting**. I **don't mind being** alone.	3. **immer** nach folgenden Verben und Ausdrücken: I can't help to keep (on) to enjoy to stop to finish to suggest to give up to be busy to go on to mind

Beachte: 1. Nach den Verben unter Punkt 2 kann auch der Infinitiv stehen.
2. Einige Gerundien sind wirkliche Substantive geworden und können einen Plural bilden:
the beginning(s) Anfang   the meeting(s)   Zusammenkunft
the crossing(s)   Überfahrt   the building(s)   Gebäude

25

Das Gerundium nach Präpositionen (The Gerund after Prepositions) § 42

Nach Präpositionen muß immer das Gerundium stehen. Merke folgende feste Verbindungen:

1. No English army was there to **prevent them from landing.** Duke William **spoke of conquering** England. Only a few ships **succeeded in escaping** to Norway.	1. **Verb + Präposition** to decide on to speak of to insist on to succeed in to look forward to to talk of (about) to prevent from to think of (about)
2. The Normans should not have **the chance of making** full use of their horsemen. Harold had the **opportunity of seeing** how many horsemen were on the Norman side.	2. **Substantiv + Präposition** the chance of for fear of the danger of the opportunity of the difficulty in the way of
3. Harold was **proud of being** king. She was not **afraid of riding** a horse.	3. **Adjektiv + Präposition** accustomed to proud of afraid of tired of fond of used to interested in

Präposition + Gerundium in der Bedeutung eines Nebensatzes § 43

Präposition + Gerundium werden im Deutschen oft durch einen adverbialen Nebensatz wiedergegeben.

Englisch: Präposition + Gerundium	Deutsch: Nebensatz
Without losing any time Harold marched northward.	Ohne Zeit zu verlieren, ...
After defeating the Norwegian army Harold hurried southward.	Nachdem Harold ... besiegt hatte, ...
By arriving in time at the cinema, we got very good seats.	Dadurch, daß wir ... ankamen, bekamen wir ...
In getting out of the bus the old lady fell.	Als sie ausstieg, ...
On walking through the City on a Sunday morning, you will not see many people.	Geht man ... durch die City, so sieht man ...

Beachte folgende Redewendungen:

How about going to the cinema?	Wie wär's, wenn wir ins Kino gingen?
What about having a cup of tea now?	Wie wär's mit einer Tasse Tee?
Our car **wants washing**.	Unser Auto muß gewaschen werden.
His hair **needs cutting**.	Sein Haar muß geschnitten werden.

11

Der bestimmte Artikel (The Definite Article) § 48

Eigennamen und Zeitbezeichnungen mit und ohne bestimmten Artikel

1. America, England, Africa, John Baker, old Mr Benson, poor Mike, Queen Elizabeth, Aunt Mary, Father, Mother	1. the USA the Netherlands the Bensons
2. Oxford Street, Hyde Park, Buckingham Palace, Tower Bridge, Scotland Yard, Dover harbour	2. the (River) Thames, the Channel, the North Sea, the Irish Sea, the Tower
3. Summer is the holiday season. an evening in July Monday is the first day of the week. on Sunday, at Easter from morning to night Lunch is at one o'clock.	3. in the morning during the afternoon through the night The lunch we had was excellent.

Ohne Artikel stehen immer

1. Eigennamen im Singular einschließlich Verwandtschaftsbezeichnungen (*Father, Mother*, etc.)
2. Ortsbezeichnungen, die mit einem Eigennamen verbunden sind
3. Zeitbezeichnungen, Monate, Wochentage, Festtage, Tageszeiten, Mahlzeiten

Mit Artikel stehen dagegen

1. Eigennamen im Plural
2. Namen von Flüssen, Meeren, Gebirgen, den meisten Bergen, einigen Gebäuden
3. Tageszeiten mit den Präpositionen *in, during, through*
   Mahlzeiten, wenn an die Speisen gedacht ist

Allgemeinbegriffe mit und ohne bestimmten Artikel § 49

1. Water is wet. My mother likes strong coffee.	1. The water we drank was cold. The coffee we had was good.
2. Dogs are faithful animals. People say he was killed. Women like beautiful dresses.	2. The dogs in the garden were barking. The people enjoyed themselves. The women in our street …
3. Life is short. Time is money. English history	3. the life of Sir Francis Drake the first time the history of England
4. School is over. Der Unterricht … Church begins at 9 o'clock. Der Gottesdienst …	4. The school was closed. Das Schulhaus … The church is open. Die Kirche …

Ohne Artikel stehen	**Mit Artikel** stehen
1. Stoffnamen	1. einzelne Sorten oder Mengen
2. Gattungsnamen im Plural, aber auch man = Mensch	2. einzelne Vertreter der Gattung
3. Abstrakta	3. Abstrakta, wenn sie näher bestimmt sind
4. Bezeichnungen für Gebäude, wenn an ihren Zweck gedacht ist	4. Bezeichnungen für die Gebäude selbst

Bestimmter Artikel bei näherer Bestimmung § 50

Substantive bekommen immer dann den Artikel, wenn sie näher bestimmt werden

1. the England of today the summer of 1588 the history of England the life of Queen Elizabeth the Church of England the Cape of Good Hope	1. durch ein nachgestelltes Attribut
2. The London (that) Shakespeare knew was much smaller than the London of today. It was the finest Christmas I ever had. The Saturday Mr Benson's class spent in Cologne was very exciting for the boys.	2. durch einen notwendigen Relativsatz

Redewendungen § 51

1. Mit bestimmtem Artikel

it is the custom	es ist Sitte	in the beginning	am Anfang, anfangs
with the exception of	mit Ausnahme von	in the end	am Ende, schließlich
with the help of	mit Hilfe von	on the whole	im großen und ganzen

2. Mit nachgestelltem Artikel

all the way	den ganzen Weg	half the size	halb so groß
both the children	beide Kinder	twice the number	zweimal so viele
double the size	doppelt so groß		

3. Ohne Artikel

at table	bei Tisch	to go to sea	zur See gehen
to be at work	bei der Arbeit sein	to go to town	in die Stadt gehen
to change colour	die Farbe wechseln	to go to work	zur Arbeit gehen
to come into fashion	Mode werden	to learn by heart	auswendig lernen
to go by car	mit dem Wagen fahren	to shake hands with s.o.	jdm. die Hand geben
to go by train	mit dem Zug fahren		

12

Der unbestimmte Artikel (The Indefinite Article)   **§ 52**

Der unbestimmte Artikel steht im Gegensatz zum Deutschen

1. fifty miles **an hour** (= every hour) ten shillings **a pound** (= each pound) The cloth costs 7 shillings **a yard**. three times **a day**	1. in der Bedeutung „je', ‚pro' bei Maßeinheiten

2. a) He was **a soldier**.
    His father is **a doctor**.
  b) Peter had become **a scout**.
  c) He is **an Englishman** and not a German.
  d) William Bradford was **a Puritan**.
	2. bei Bezeichnungen für
	  a) Beruf
	  b) Mitgliedschaft
	  c) Nationalität
	
	  d) Religion
	besonders nach *to be* und *to become*

Beachte: Der unbestimmte Artikel steht jedoch nicht bei Berufsbezeichnungen und Titeln, die nur **einer** Person zukommen: She became Queen of England.

Redewendungen:

to be at an end	am Ende sein	to have a temperature	Fieber haben
to be at a loss	in Verlegenheit sein	to make a noise	Lärm machen
to be in a hurry	in Eile sein	to speak in a low voice	mit leiser Stimme sprechen
to have a cold	Schnupfen haben		
to have a headache	Kopfschmerzen haben	to take a seat	Platz nehmen, sich hinsetzen
to have an opportunity	Gelegenheit haben		

Nachstellung des unbestimmten Artikels   **§ 53**
(The Indefinite Article in the End Position)

Der unbestimmte Artikel wird nachgestellt bei

1. **half an** hour **quite a** small community **rather a** difficult question **such a** gale **What a** fine boy!	1. half halb quite recht, ganz, ziemlich rather ziemlich such solch, so ein what Was für (ein) ...!
2. She was **as good a teacher as** her sister. The Pilgrims had never made **so long a journey**. It is **too long a story** to tell you now. **However hard a winter** it is, spring will come. Wie streng der Winter auch sein mag, ...	2. Adjektiven, die mit *as ... as, so, too, how, however* verbunden sind

13

Die einfache Form und die Verlaufsform des Perfekts   § 54
(The Present Perfect Ordinary and Continuous)   *since or for*

1. The window is open. Who **has opened** it? – I have. Wer hat es aufgemacht?	1. Das Present Perfect Ordinary bezeichnet einen Vorgang in der Vergangenheit, dessen Folgen für die Gegenwart noch Bedeutung haben. Im Deutschen steht das Perfekt.
2. I **have been waiting** since 10 o'clock (and he still is not here). Ich warte schon seit … They **have been working** on my car for two hours (and it still does not run). Sie arbeiten schon seit zwei Stunden (zwei Stunden lang) …	2. Das Present Perfect Ordinary oder Continuous bezeichnet in Verbindung mit Zeitangaben (z. B. *since Monday*, *for two weeks* usw.) einen Vorgang, der von der Vergangenheit bis in die Gegenwart reicht. – Die Continuous Form wird bevorzugt. Im Deutschen steht meist das Präsens + ‚schon'.

Folgende Verben bilden meist keine Continuous Form:

a) Verben der Wahrnehmung: to hear; to notice; to see; to smell; to taste
b) Verben der Zu- und Abneigung: to like; to dislike; to hate; to love; to mind; to prefer
c) Verben des Wünschens: to want; to wish
d) Verben des Glaubens und Meinens: to agree; to believe; to remember; to doubt; to feel (that …); to know; to understand
e) einige Verben, die einen Zustand bezeichnen: to be; to belong; to contain; to have (= besitzen); to possess

Das deutsche ‚seit'   § 55

Das deutsche ‚seit' wird wiedergegeben

1. I haven't seen her **since Monday**. He has been living here **since 1945**. It has been raining **since yesterday morning**.	1. durch *since* = seit bei Angabe eines Zeitpunkts
2. We have been learning English **for three years now**. I haven't seen Peter **for at least two months**. Mrs Miller has been ill **for a long time**.	2. durch *for* = seit bei Angabe eines Zeitraums

Die einfache Form und die Verlaufsform des Plusquamperfekts § 56
(The Past Perfect Ordinary and Continuous)

Present Perfect (Bezugspunkt: Gegenwart)	Past Perfect (Bezugspunkt: Vergangenheit)
We are very hungry because **we haven't had** anything to eat for two days. Mary is very happy because **she has just heard** some good news.	We were very hungry when we arrived because **we had not had** anything to eat for two days. Mary was very happy when she came to see me because **she had just heard** some good news.
He has been walking through the streets for five hours and is tired now. **He has been working** on his new book for two years now.	**He had been walking** through the streets for five hours when I met him at Victoria Station. **He had been working** on a new book for two years but then he suddenly gave it up.

14

Das Konditional II der Hilfsverben (vgl. § 19) § 57
(The Conditional Perfect of the Auxiliaries)

	Konditional I	Konditional II
can	You **could** wait. Du könntest warten.	You **could have waited.** Du hättest warten können.
may	You **might** wait. Du könntest warten.	You **might have waited.** Du hättest warten können.
must	Ersatzverb: You **would have to** wait. Du müßtest warten.	Ersatzverb: You **would have had to** wait. Du hättest warten müssen.
shall	You **should** wait. You **ought to** wait. Du solltest warten.	You **should have waited.** You **ought to have waited.** Du hättest warten sollen.
will	**Would** you **wait?** Würdest du warten?	**Would** you **have waited?** Würdest du gewartet haben? Hättest du gewartet?

Das Konditional II der Hilfsverben wird gebildet, indem man das Vollverb in den Infinitiv Perfekt setzt.

Englische Entsprechungen deutscher modaler Hilfsverben

Beide Sprachen verfügen über verschiedene Möglichkeiten, das Können, Dürfen, Müssen, Sollen und Wollen zum Ausdruck zu bringen.

1. Das Können § 58

He can swim well. Do you know French? He can speak French. Our teacher can be strict.	können	dauernde Fähigkeit oder Eigenschaft
Is he able to come today? Today he is unable to come.	in der Lage sein	Fähigkeit zu einem bestimmten Augenblick
The report may be true. It might be right. It could be right.	vielleicht können	Möglichkeit

2. Das Dürfen § 59

Might I use your pen? May I come in? – Yes, you may. Can I come in? – Yes, you can.	dürfen	Erlaubnis
... No, you may not. ... No, you can't. He was not allowed to stay.	nicht dürfen	von einer einzelnen Person ausgehendes Verbot
You mustn't smoke in here.	verboten sein	allgemein gültiges Verbot

3. Das Müssen § 60

Must you go soon? I have to get up early in the morning.	müssen	Verpflichtung, Zwang
It must be rather late.	es muß ...	Vermutung
You need not help me. You don't have to wait for me.	nicht brauchen, nicht müssen	keine Verpflichtung

4. Das Sollen § 61

Shall I buy some ham?	sollen	Weisung
You ought to help your mother.	(eigentlich) sollen	moralische Verpflichtung
You should see a doctor. If you should meet him, tell him ...	solltest	Gebot Möglichkeit
We are to be there at 9 o'clock.	sollen	Verpflichtung, Auftrag

5. Das Wollen §62

I want to finish my work first.	wollen	Absicht
They are going to leave England.	im Begriff sein	
I intend to buy a new car.	beabsichtigen	
He wished to go to America. We should like to leave now.	} gern wollen	Wunsch
I will come tonight, but I won't stay.	wollen	Wille, meist nur in der 1. Person
Will you buy me a newspaper, please? — Yes, I will.	willst du ..., bitte ...	Bitte, nur in der 2. Person

15

Das Possessivpronomen (The Possessive Adjective and Pronoun) §63

Formen:

adjektivisch *(Possessive Adjective)*	substantivisch *(Possessive Pronoun)*		
I like **my** book(s).	I likes **mine** best.	das (die) meinige(n)
You like **your** book(s).	You likes **yours** best.	das (die) deinige(n)
He likes **his** book(s).	He likes **his** best.	das (die) seinige(n)
She likes **her** book(s).	She likes **hers** best.	das (die) ihrige(n)
The dog likes **its** basket.	It likes **its own** best.	den seinigen
We like **our** book(s).	We like **ours** best.	das (die) unsrige(n)
You like **your** book(s).	You like **yours** best.	das (die) eurige(n)
They like **their** book(s).	They like **theirs** best.	das (die) ihrige(n)

Beachte das unpersönliche Possessivpronomen:

adjektivisch: One should always do **one's** best.   Man sollte immer sein Bestes tun.
substantivisch: One shouldn't use anybody else's pen
                   but **one's own**.   ..., sondern seinen eigenen.

Das adjektivische Possessivpronomen (The Possessive Adjective) §64

Im Gegensatz zum Deutschen steht im Englischen das adjektivische Possessivpronomen

| a) They washed **their** hands and **their** faces.
    ... die Hände und das Gesicht.
b) Take off **your** hat.
    ... den Hut
c) He lost **his** life in a fire.
    ... das Leben | a) bei Bezeichnungen für Körperteile
b) bei Bezeichnungen für Kleidungsstücke
c) bei Wörtern wie *life*, *mind* und *death* |

Redewendungen:

to change one's mind	sich anders besinnen	to hold one's breath	den Atem anhalten
to make up one's mind	sich entschließen	with all one's heart	von ganzem Herzen
to lose one's head	den Kopf verlieren	I beg your pardon.	Wie bitte? Verzeihung!
to find one's way	den Weg finden	It is my turn.	Ich bin an der Reihe.

Das substantivische Possessivpronomen (The Possessive Pronoun) § 65

Das substantivische Possessivpronomen hat für Singular und Plural dieselbe Form. Es steht

1. Let's tell stories. I'll tell you **mine** and you tell me **yours**. ... meine (die meinigen), ... deine (die deinigen). If your car is too small, we can take **ours**. **Ours** is much larger than **yours**.	1. im Gegensatz zum Deutschen ohne Artikel
2. Is this book **yours**? Gehört dieses Buch dir? No, it is not **mine**. Nein, es gehört mir nicht. I think these sun-glasses are **yours**. Ich glaube, diese Sonnenbrille gehört dir.	2. mit einer Form von *to be* im Sinne von ‚gehören'

Beachte: 1. Bei Substantiven wird das substantivische Possessivpronomen nachgestellt:
　　　　　He is **a friend of mine.** (= one of my friends)
　　　　　Some cows of his were ill with cow-pox. (= some of his cows)

　　　　2. Auch der s-Genitiv kann hinter dem Substantiv stehen:
　　　　　A friend of my father's is living in Africa. (= one of my father's friends)
　　　　　Those people are **friends of Mr Miller's.** (= Mr Miller's friends)

Das verstärkende 'own' (The emphatic 'own') § 66

She makes **her own** dresses.	Sie näht ihre Kleider selbst.
I do **my own** shopping.	Ich gehe selbst einkaufen.
He offered **his own** son for the experiment.	... seinen eigenen Sohn
My sister goes to work in **her own** car.	... in ihrem eigenen Wagen
Each village has **its own** school.	Jedes Dorf hat seine eigene Schule.

Das adjektivische Possessivpronomen kann durch *own* verstärkt werden.

Beachte: Vor *own* muß immer ein Possessivpronomen stehen:
　　　　　I have a theory **of my own.** ... eine eigene Theorie
　　　　　My brother has a room **of his own.** ... ein eigenes Zimmer
　　　　　We have a house **of our own.** ... ein eigenes Haus

16

Die Verlaufsform des Präsens mit futurischer Bedeutung § 67
(The Continuous Form of the Present Tense used in a Future Sense)

1. **I'm leaving** New York next week. Nächste Woche werde ich von New York abreisen.	1. Das Präsens der Verlaufsform *(Present Continuous)* kann eine zukünftige Handlung bezeichnen. (Immer mit Zeitangabe.)
2. That is exactly what **I'm going to do**. Genau das werde ich tun. They **are going to be** married. Sie werden heiraten.	2. *to be going* + Infinitiv bezeichnet eine beabsichtigte Handlung, die mit Gewißheit oder Wahrscheinlichkeit eintreten wird.

Das deutsche „man" § 68

Das deutsche „man" kann im Englischen wiedergegeben werden

1. **One** never knows. Man kann nie wissen. In California **you** could become rich. ... konnte man In 1848 **they** found gold in California. ... fand man **People** led a wild life in the Golden West. Man führte ...	1. durch one you they people
2. English **is spoken** all over the world. Überall in der Welt spricht man Englisch.	2. durch das Passiv

17

Verben ohne und mit Objekt (Verbs without and with an Object) § 69

ohne Objekt	mit Objekt
My new car **runs** smoothly. Mein neuer Wagen läuft ruhig. The plane **flies** to New York. Die Maschine fliegt nach New York.	I **ran the car** into the garage. Ich fuhr den Wagen in die Garage. The pilot **flew his plane** across the ocean. Der Pilot flog seine Maschine über den Ozean.

Manche Verben, die gewöhnlich kein Objekt haben, können mit direktem Objekt verbunden werden (veranlassende Verben). Dazu gehören:

to drop	to grow	to race	to sail	to stand
to fly	to march	to run	to sink	to work

Passiv bei Verben mit präpositionalem Objekt § 70
(Verb + Preposition + Object in the Passive)

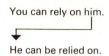

Nobody likes **being laughed at.** Niemand hat es gern, wenn über ihn gelacht wird. Such things **had** never **been heard of** before. So etwas hatte man noch nie zuvor gehört. Here they **will be** well **taken care of.** Hier wird gut für sie gesorgt werden. His ideas **were** often **made fun of.** Man machte sich oft über seine Ideen lustig. The plane **was** soon **lost sight of.** Das Flugzeug war bald außer Sicht.	Viele englische Verben und verbale Ausdrücke sind so fest mit einer Präposition verbunden, daß diese feste Verbindung im Passiv bestehen bleibt.

Dazu gehören:

to agree (up)on	to look (up)on	to lose sight of
to arrive at	to pay for	to make fun of
to ask for	to rely on	to make the most of
to depend on	to send for	to make use of
to dream of	to smile at	to pay attention to
to hear of	to speak about (of, to)	to put an end to
to laugh at	to talk about (of, to)	to take advantage of
to listen to	to tell about (of)	to take care of
to look after (at, for)	to think about (of)	to wait for

18

Die prädikative Ergänzung (The Predicative Complement) § 71

Subjekt		Präd.Ergänzung	Objekt		Präd.Ergänzung
a) **He**	was	**angry.**	b) The news made **him**		**angry.**
Stephenson	became	**chief engineer.**	They appointed **Stephenson**		**chief engineer.**

Die prädikative Ergänzung kann ein Adjektiv oder ein Substantiv sein. Sie bezeichnet eine Eigenschaft des Subjekts oder Objekts.

a) Die prädikative Ergänzung zum Subjekt steht bei folgenden Verben: § 72

The girls became **friends**.	to be	sein	to smell	riechen
That record remained **safe** for over 30 years.	to seem to appear }	scheinen	to taste to sound	schmecken klingen
The children kept **quiet**. We felt **tired** when we came back from the walk.	to remain to keep to feel	} bleiben sich (an)fühlen	to become to get (dark) to grow (old) }	werden
He turned **pale** when he read the telegram. She looked **pretty** in her new dress.	to look	aussehen	to turn (pale)	

Merke folgende feste Verbindungen:

to come true sich bestätigen, sich erfüllen   to go wrong schiefgehen
to fall ill krank werden   to go mad verrückt werden

b) Die prädikative Ergänzung zum Objekt steht § 73

1. I find this book **very interesting**. They made him **their leader**.	1. ohne Präposition bei to appoint ernennen (zu) to find finden, daß to crown krönen (zu) to make machen (zu) to declare erklären (zu) to think halten (für)
2. Thousands who had taken the railways **for gold mines** were ruined. They regarded this record **as unbeatable**.	2. mit *as* bzw. *for* bei to acknowledge as to recognize as } anerkennen als to take for halten für to regard as betrachten als to look (up)on as ansehen als
3. I had always considered him **(as) a great artist**. They elected him **(as) president**.	3. mit oder ohne *as* bzw. *for* bei to choose (as, for) (aus)wählen zu to consider (as) betrachten als to elect (as) wählen zu

Das Partizip als prädikative Ergänzung § 74
(The Participle as Predicative Complement)

Das Partizip steht als prädikative Ergänzung

1. **They stood** there **looking** at the ship.
   Sie standen da und schauten ...
   He came running down the stairs.
   Er kam ... gelaufen
	1. zum Subjekt nach
	to come to sit
	to go to stand
	to lie to stay
	to remain

2. When we came to the river we **noticed a man swimming** across. ... sahen wir einen Mann schwimmen I entered the house and **heard two men talking** to each other. ... hörte zwei Männer miteinander reden	2. zum Objekt nach den Verben der Wahrnehmung to feel to see to hear to watch to notice

Beachte zu 2.: Nach den Verben der Wahrnehmung kann statt des Partizip Präsens auch der Infinitiv ohne *to* stehen:
    I **saw a man swim** across the river.   Ich sah einen Mann über den Fluß schwimmen.

Das deutsche „lassen"   § 75

Unterscheide:

1. As he was tired we **let him sleep**. ... ließen wir ihn schlafen. Don't **let the dog come** into the kitchen. Laß den Hund nicht in die Küche!	1. zulassen = *to let* + Infinitiv ohne *to*
2. a) This **made the public change** its attitude towards the railways. Das veranlaßte die Öffentlichkeit, ihre Einstellung der Eisenbahn gegenüber zu ändern. She **had the servant lay** the table. Sie ließ den Diener den Tisch decken. b) France **had** new electric **locomotives built**. Frankreich ließ neue elektrische Lokomotiven bauen. Go and **get your hair cut**. Laß dir die Haare schneiden!	2. veranlassen, a) daß jemand etwas tut = *to make, to have* + Infinitiv ohne *to* b) daß etwas getan wird = *to have, to get* + Partizip Perfekt
3. I **left my umbrella** in the train. Ich habe meinen Schirm im Zug liegenlassen.	3. zurücklassen = *to leave*

19

Adverbiale Bestimmungen beim Present Perfect   § 76
(Adverbial Phrases with the Present Perfect)

Have you ever **been** to Scotland? **Have** you **seen** Mike recently? **Has** John **arrived** yet? I **have been** here now for a week.	Bist du jemals in Schottland gewesen? Hast du Mike in letzter Zeit gesehen? Ist John schon angekommen? Ich bin jetzt seit einer Woche hier.

Das Present Perfect steht bei Zeitangaben, die eine Beziehung zur Gegenwart haben:

already	this morning (week, year, etc.)
(during) all these years	today
ever	up to this moment
just	yet (in Frage und Verneinung)
recently	since Monday ⎫
so far	for a week ⎭ = seit

Stellung von 'so' §77

Um den Inhalt eines vorhergehenden Satzes wieder aufzunehmen, verwendet man im Englischen bei bestimmten Verben *so* = dt. ‚es', ‚das'.

1. "Has Mother come back yet?" – "I believe so." „Ist Mutter schon zurück?" – „Ich glaube ja." "Is it going to rain?" – "Oh yes, I think so." „Wird es regnen?" – „Ich denke." "Is he in the office?" – "I suppose so." „Ist er im Büro?" – „Ich nehme es an."	1. *so* folgt dem Verb bei to believe to say to expect to suppose to hope to think
2. "John has been here." – "So I hear." „John war hier." – „Das habe ich gehört." "I have broken a plate." – "So I see." „Ich habe einen Teller zerschlagen." – „Das sehe ich."	2. *so* steht an der Satzspitze bei den Verben to hear to see to notice

20

Die indirekte Rede (Reported Speech) §78

Direkte Rede	Indirekte Rede	
"I want to do something useful."	She says (that) she wants to do something useful. ..., daß sie ... wolle. ..., sie wolle ...	Im Englischen steht abweichend vom Deutschen in der indirekten Rede stets der Indikativ. *That* kann weggelassen werden.
"Can I do something useful?"	She asks if she can do something useful. ..., ob sie ... könne.	

Beachte: 1. Vor der indirekten Rede steht kein Komma.
            2. Als indirekte Rede gelten auch Sätze nach folgenden Verben:

to be afraid	to believe	to hope	to think
to be sure	to fear	to know	to wonder

Die Zeitenfolge in der indirekten Rede § 79
(The Sequence of Tenses in Reported Speech)

Das Verb der indirekten Rede richtet sich nach der Zeitform des einführenden Satzes. Dabei unterscheidet man zwei Gruppen:
a) **Gegenwartsgruppe** (Present, Present Perfect)
b) **Vergangenheitsgruppe** (Past, Past Perfect)

a) Einführungssatz: Gegenwartsgruppe

Direkte Rede	Indirekte Rede
"All our friends **will look** down on us."	She **says** (that) all our friends **will look** down on us.
"**I'm leaving** tonight."	He **has** just **told** me (that) **he is leaving** tonight.

Steht der Einführungssatz in einer Zeitform der Gegenwartsgruppe, so wird in der indirekten Rede die Zeitform der direkten Rede beibehalten.

b) Einführungssatz: Vergangenheitsgruppe

Direkte Rede	Indirekte Rede
Present Tense →	Past Tense
"I **want** to work in a hospital."	Florence **said** to her mother (that) she **wanted** to work in a hospital.
Present Perfect →	Past Perfect
"I **have read** this book already."	He **told** me (that) he **had read** that book already.
Past Tense →	Past Perfect
"Mr Brown **spent** several years in the USA."	Peter **said** (that) Mr Brown **had spent** several years in the USA.
Future Tense →	Conditional
"I **shall make** preparations at once."	She **had said** (that) she **would make** preparations at once.

Beachte zu b: Bei der Umwandlung der direkten in die indirekte Rede wird

this	zu	that	yesterday	zu	the day before
these	zu	those	last week	zu	the week before
here	zu	there	a week ago	zu	a week before
now	zu	then	today	zu	that day
tomorrow	zu	the next day	next week	zu	the following week

Der Fragesatz in der indirekten Rede § 80
(Questions in Reported Speech)

Direkte Rede	Indirekte Rede
"When does the plane for New York take off?"	The policeman asks when the plane for New York takes off.
"Where did you buy this dress?"	Dorothy asks where I bought this dress.
"Who is living in the house next to yours?"	The man has just asked me who is living in the house next to ours.
"Do you believe me or not?"	She asked whether I believed her or not.
"Are you willing to go to the Crimea?"	Mr Herbert asked Florence if she was willing to go to the Crimea.
"Why didn't you come to the meeting?"	She asked why I hadn't come to the meeting.

Beachte: Der indirekte Fragesatz hat die Wortstellung S-P-O des Aussagesatzes.

Der Imperativ in der indirekten Rede § 81
(The Imperative in Reported Speech)

Der Imperativ wird in der indirekten Rede wiedergegeben

Direkte Rede	Indirekte Rede	
1. "Send more nurses from England." "Don't wait for me." "Take the suitcases downstairs and call a taxi for me, please."	1. Florence asked Mr Herbert to send more nurses from England. He told us not to wait for him. Mr Brown asked me to take the suitcases downstairs and to call a taxi for him.	1. durch einen Infinitiv
2. "Shut the door behind you." "Return to England, Florence." "Don't tell anybody what you have seen."	2. He said (that) we must shut the door behind us. Florence's friends told her (that) she should return to England. He said (that) I should not tell anybody what I had seen.	2. durch einen Satz mit *must* oder *should*

21

Besonderheiten beim Adverb
Adjektive auf -ly   § 82

Adjektiv	Adverb
1. She is a **friendly** girl. 2. He took an **early** train. He reads a **daily** and a **weekly** newspaper.	1. She talks **in a friendly way**. 2. Oates got up **early**. Does this newspaper come **daily** or **weekly**?

1. Die Adjektive auf *-ly* bilden kein Adverb. Ersatz dafür sind Umschreibungen: in a ... way; in a ... manner.
2. Die Zeitadjektive *early, daily, weekly, monthly, yearly* werden unverändert auch als Adverbien verwendet.

Adjektiv und Adverb haben dieselbe Form   § 83
1. bei gleicher Bedeutung

Adjektiv	Adverb
My uncle has a **fast** car. ... ein schnelles Auto. They spent the **long** polar winter in the camp. ... den langen Polarwinter I want **half** a pound of coffee. ... ein halbes Pfund Kaffee. Look at this **straight** row of houses. ... gerade Reihe von Häusern. He has a **low** voice. ... eine tiefe Stimme.	His health was sinking **fast**. ... verschlechterte sich schnell. We didn't stay **long**. Wir blieben nicht lange. The potatoes were only **half** cooked. ... nur halb gekocht. He cannot walk **straight** any more. ... gerade laufen. The plane is flying **low**. ... fliegt tief.

2. bei verschiedener Bedeutung

Adjektiv	Adverb
Jack seems to be **ill**. Jack scheint krank zu sein. This is the **only** pair of shoes I have. ... das einzige Paar Schuhe ... He is not quite **well** today. ... nicht ganz gesund.	Don't think **ill** of him. Denke nicht schlecht von ihm. I have **only** 10 shillings left. Ich habe nur noch 10 Shilling. You did very **well** in your test. ... sehr gut gemacht.

Adverb mit und ohne -ly §84

1. bei gleicher oder ähnlicher Bedeutung

Adverb ohne -*ly*		Adverb mit -*ly*	
to buy **cheap**	billig kaufen	He got it **cheaply**.	... billig
to sell **cheap**	billig verkaufen		
to speak **loud**	laut sprechen	He laughed **loudly**.	... laut
to guess **right**	richtig raten	He is **rightly** punished.	... zu Recht
to go **wrong**	fehlgehen	He is **wrongly** punished.	... zu Unrecht

2. bei verschiedener Bedeutung

Adverb ohne -*ly*		Adverb mit -*ly*	
to sink **deep**	tief sinken	He was **deeply** hurt.	... schwer gekränkt
to play **fair**	fair spielen	He plays **fairly** well.	... ziemlich gut
to work **hard**	schwer arbeiten	He **hardly** works.	... kaum
to fly **high**	hoch fliegen	He is **highly** paid.	... gut
to arrive **late**	spät ankommen	Have you seen him **lately**?	... kürzlich
to be **pretty** good	ziemlich gut sein	She dresses **prettily**.	... hübsch
to stop **short**	plötzlich stehenbleiben	He arrived **shortly** afterwards.	... kurz danach
to run **short**	zu Ende gehen	He will come **shortly**.	... in Kürze
to sell **dear**	teuer verkaufen	We loved him **dearly**.	... herzlich

Englisches Verb statt deutschem Adverb §85

I'd like to go to the South Pole myself one day.	Ich möchte selbst **gern** einmal zum Südpol fahren.
I offered to drive him home, but he **preferred** to walk.	... wollte **lieber** zu Fuß gehen.
They **happened** to discover marks in the snow.	Sie entdeckten **zufällig** Spuren im Schnee.
He is sure to come tomorrow. **I'm sure he** will come tomorrow.	Er wird **sicher (bestimmt)** morgen kommen.

Oft entsprechen englische Verben deutschen Adverbien:

to like to to love to to be fond of	gern	to go on (+ Ger.) to keep (on) (+ Ger.) to continue (+ Inf. od. Ger.)	weiter, dauernd
to prefer to to like better	lieber	to seem to to be likely to	anscheinend wahrscheinlich
to happen to	zufällig	to be sure to	sicher, bestimmt

22

Der Infinitiv ohne 'to' als Teil des direkten Objekts (AcI) § 86
(vgl. § 74) (The Infinitive without 'to' as Part of the Direct Object—AcI)

	Objekt	
	Akkusativ	Infinitiv
1. They saw Sie sahen	**a man** einen Mann	**disappear** round the corner. um die Ecke verschwinden.
2. He lets Er läßt They made Sie ließen She had Sie ließ	**the dog** den Hund **him** ihn **the servant** den Diener	**sleep** in his room. in seinem Zimmer schlafen. **pay** for his mistake. für seinen Fehler büßen. **lock** all the doors. alle Türen abschließen.

Der Infinitiv ohne *to* steht als Teil des Objekts (Objektsfall = Akkusativ)

1. nach Verben der Wahrnehmung: to feel, to hear, to notice, to see, to watch
2. nach to make (veran)lassen; zwingen
      to have (veran)lassen; sagen, daß ... soll
      to let (zu)lassen

Beachte: AcI = lat. Accusativus cum Infinitivo (Akkusativ mit Infinitiv)

Der Infinitiv mit 'to' als Teil des direkten Objekts (AcI) § 87
(The Infinitive with 'to' as Part of the Direct Object—AcI)

	Objekt	
	Akkusativ	Infinitiv
1. He wanted Er wollte, daß Father hates Vater mag es nicht, wenn	**them** sie **us** wir	**to be** resourceful. wendig seien. **to come** home late. spät nach Hause kommen.
2. He expected Er erwartete, daß The fisherman warned Der Fischer warnte	**everybody** jeder **the boys** die Jungen davor,	**to do** his work. seine Arbeit tat. **not to swim** out too far. zu weit hinauszuschwimmen.
3. He knew Er wußte, daß	**the examination** das Examen	**to contain** a difficult test in mathematics. ... enthielt.

Der Infinitiv mit *to* steht als Teil des Objekts
1. Nach Verben des Wünschens und Nichtwünschens:
to hate	to want	I should prefer
to like	to wish	
2. Nach Verben des Veranlassens, Forderns und Zulassens:
to allow	to expect	to warn (not to . . .)
to ask	to order	
to cause	to tell	

   Im Deutschen steht bei einigen Verben dieselbe Konstruktion, sonst Nebensatz mit ‚daß'.
3. Nach Verben des Vermutens, allerdings nur in der geschriebenen Sprache:
to believe	to know	to think
to consider	to suppose	

Passiver Infinitiv des AcI (The Passive Infinitive of the AcI) § 88

Aktiver Infinitiv	Passiver Infinitiv
He **ordered the boys to dig** trenches. (= The boys dug trenches.) Er gab den Jungen den Auftrag, Gräben auszuheben. I **want you to send** the mail to my hotel.	He **ordered trenches to be dug.** (= Trenches were dug.) Er gab den Auftrag, Gräben auszuheben. I **want the mail to be sent** to my hotel.

Hat der Infinitiv passiven Sinn, so steht im Englischen die passive Form des Infinitivs.

Der Infinitiv nach passivem Prädikat (NcI) § 89
(The Infinitive after Verbs in the Passive Voice)

AcI: His father made him work hard.

NcI: He was made to work hard.

Wird ein Satz, der einen AcI enthält, ins Passiv verwandelt, so wird der Akkusativ zum Subjekt des Satzes. Aus dem AcI (Akkusativ mit Infinitiv) wird ein NcI (Nominativ mit Infinitiv).

> This story **is believed to be** true. Man glaubt, die Geschichte sei wahr.
> He **was said to be** 'only average'. Man sagte, er sei ‚nur Durchschnitt'.
> The Boers **were seen to win** one battle after another. Man sah . . . gewinnen.
> She **was supposed to be** here at 10 o'clock. Sie hätte um 10 Uhr hier sein sollen.

Der mit einem passiven Prädikat verbundene Infinitiv (immer mit *to*) steht häufig nach folgenden Verben:

to be believed to	to be known to	to be supposed to
to be considered to	to be said to	
to be expected to	to be seen to	

Alphabetisches Verzeichnis grammatischer Ausdrücke

adjective	ˈædʒiktiv	Adjektiv
adverb	ˈædvəːb	Adverb
adverbial phrase	ədˈvəːbiəl ˈfreiz	adverbiale Bestimmung
affirmative	əˈfəːmətiv	bejahend
article	ˈɑːtikl	Artikel
auxiliary verb	ɔːgˈziljəri ˈvəːb	Hilfsverb
cardinal number	ˈkɑːdinl ˈnʌmbə	Grundzahl
case	keis	Kasus, Fall
clause	klɔːz	Satz
comma	ˈkɔmə	Komma
comparative	kəmˈpærətiv	Komparativ
comparison	kəmˈpærisn	Steigerung
compound	ˈkɔmpaund	Zusammensetzung
compound noun	ˈkɔmpaund ˈnaun	zusammengesetztes Substantiv
conditional	kənˈdiʃnl	Konditional I
conditional clause	kənˈdiʃnl ˈklɔːz	Bedingungssatz
conditional perfect	kənˈdiʃnl ˈpəːfikt	Konditional II
conjunction	kənˈdʒʌŋkʃən	Konjunktion
consonant	ˈkɔnsənənt	Konsonant
continuous form	kənˈtinjuəs ˈfɔːm	Verlaufsform
defective auxiliary verb	diˈfektiv ɔːgˈziljəri ˈvəːb	unvollständiges Hilfsverb
defining relative clause	diˈfainiŋ ˈrelətiv ˈklɔːz	notwendiger Relativsatz
definite article	ˈdefinit ˈɑːtikl	bestimmter Artikel
demonstrative pronoun	diˈmɔnstrətiv ˈprounaun	Demonstrativpronomen
direct object	ˈdairekt ˈɔbdʒikt	direktes Objekt
emphatic	imˈfætik	verstärkend
future	ˈfjuːtʃə	Futur
gender	ˈdʒendə	Geschlecht
genitive	ˈdʒenitiv	Genitiv
gerund	ˈdʒerənd	Gerundium
imperative	imˈperətiv	Imperativ
indefinite article	inˈdefinit ˈɑːtikl	unbestimmter Artikel
indefinite pronoun	inˈdefinit ˈprounaun	unbestimmtes Pronomen
indirect object	ˈindiˌrect ˈɔbdʒikt	indirektes Objekt
infinitive	inˈfinitiv	Infinitiv
interrogative	intəˈrɔgətiv	Fragewort
interrogative pronoun	intəˈrɔgətiv ˈprounaun	Fragepronomen
irregular verb	iˈregjulə ˈvəːb	unregelmäßiges Verb
main clause	ˈmein ˈklɔːz	Hauptsatz
measure	ˈmeʒə	Maß
negative	ˈnegətiv	verneinend
non-defining relative clause	ˈnɔndiˈfainiŋ ˈrelətiv ˈklɔːz	ausmalender Relativsatz
noun	naun	Substantiv
number	ˈnʌmbə	Zahl(enangabe)
numeral	ˈnjuːmərəl	Zahlwort